Meditating Your Way to a Great Big Smile!

A Beginner's Guide to Meditation for Little Ones

Ana Cybela

Illustrations by Widya Arumba

Copyright © 2021 by Ana Cybela

All rights reserved. No part of this book may be reproduced or used in any manner without written permission of the copyright owner except for the use of quotations in a book review or for educational purposes.

Printed in the United States

Paperback ISBN: 978-1-955105-03-3
Hardback ISBN: 978-1-955105-05-7

For Sophie and Zoe

Waking Up

It is time to **wake up** your body and your mind.

Find somewhere to sit comfortably. Close your eyes. Imagine the **sun** is rising above you and is shining brightly on your face.

In your imagination, see the sunlight shining on every **animal** and **plant** on earth, providing energy for all to grow and thrive. Breathe in and out slowly. Feel the warmth on your face, stretch, and smile.

Good morning, **world**. The light in me sees the light in you.

Feeling Energized

You may still feel a little **tired** and that is okay.

Take a moment to slowly wake your body up.
Gently close your eyes. Take a deep breath in, and when you exhale,
stretch your arms and imagine a pair of wings on your back.

In your mind, see the wings start beating, slow and strong.
They lift you up, taking you higher and higher, closer and closer
to the white fluffy clouds. Feel the wind on your face.
I am ready for a brand new day.

Letting Go of Worry

You may be **worried** about something that's happening later today, like a test, or a challenging school project. It is perfectly normal to feel worry or stress sometimes.

Spend a moment preparing for your day. Take a few deep breaths in through your nose and out through your mouth.

Each time you exhale, imagine blowing air on a white fluffy dandelion puffball.

Name each of your worries and watch them float away like little dandelion **seeds**.

I let go of worry and do the best that I can. Mistakes teach me ways to **grow**.

Looking at Things From a Different Angle

A lot of things will happen throughout your day. Some things might make you feel happy and excited, and some things might make you worried and stressed. It is perfectly normal, and it is okay.

Take a moment and close your eyes. Imagine throwing a **rock** into a little **creek** and watching it create a big ripple.

Breathe in deeply, and as you breathe out, throw the same rock into a big **ocean**. The ripple is much smaller this time, and you can hardly see it.

When I grow **bigger**, my problems become **smaller**.

Spreading Kindness

It is lunchtime. Is there someone sitting **alone** at the cafeteria? Today, go up to that person and ask if you can join them for lunch.

Clearing the Mind

Throughout your day, there may be lots of things to do and look at. So many classes, books, projects, and other interesting things. It is perfectly normal to feel a little **lost**.

Take a moment to find your focus. Close your eyes gently and imagine you are in front of a huge aquarium full of colorful **fish**. There is so much to see. Take a deep breath in through your nose and fill your stomach with air, like a balloon. Then blow all the air out through your mouth.

Focus on one fish at a time and see how they slowly form a seamless **circle**, swimming peacefully in one direction. I choose to stay in the present moment and focus on **one** thing at a time.

Creating Space

Every day you are learning about new things. Some things are exciting and interesting, while some may seem complicated and hard to understand.

You may feel **frustrated** or **overwhelmed**. It is perfectly normal. Everyone feels this way sometimes.

Find a moment to close your eyes and take a deep breath in.
When you blow the air out through your mouth,
imagine yourself coloring a giant flower mandala
in any colors you can think of. Examine these colors closely.

As you keep breathing in and out, smile and watch
as the beautiful flower blooms in the full spectrum of vibrant colors.

I am the master of my own mind.
I create space for new things to grow.

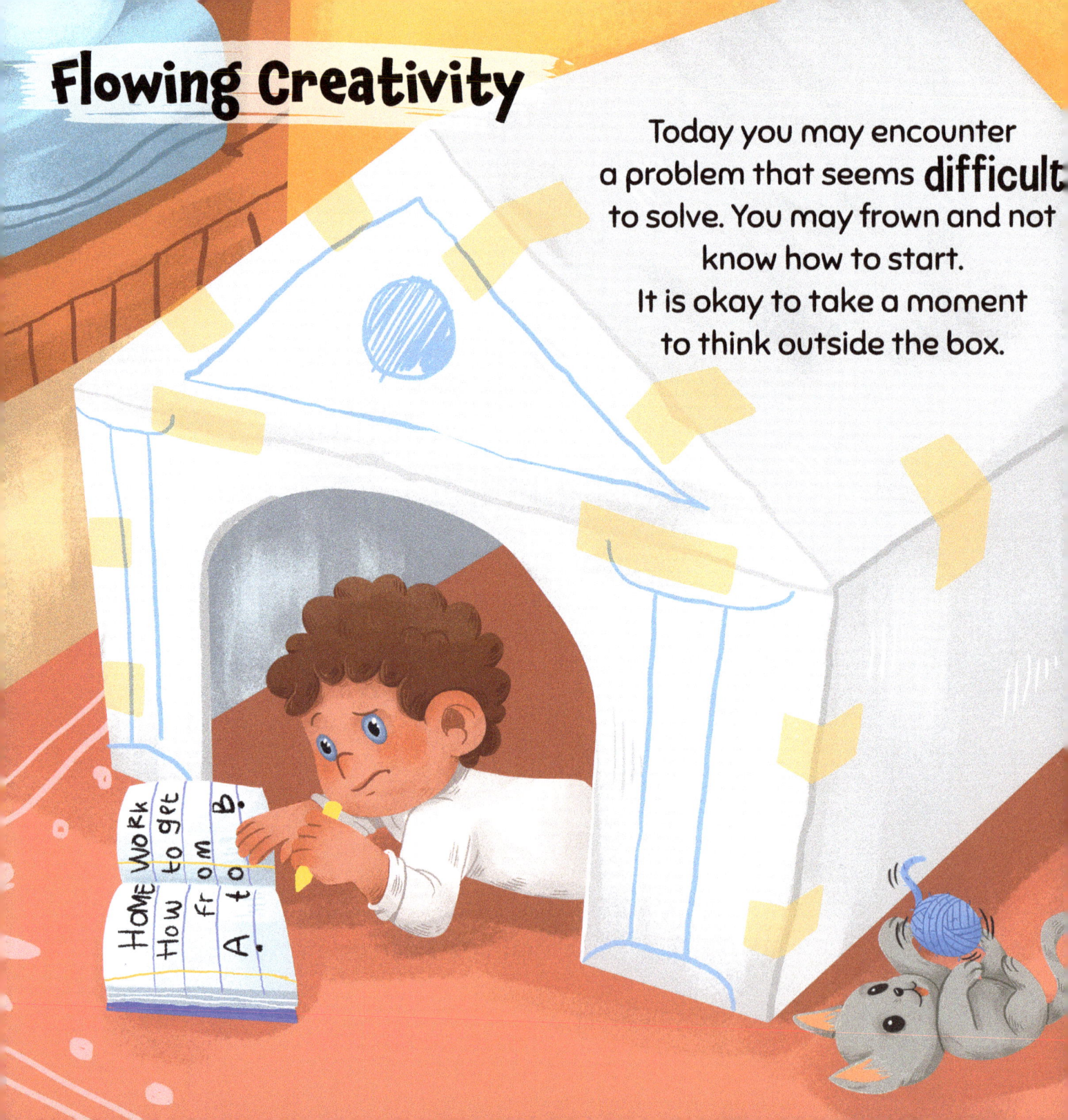

Flowing Creativity

Today you may encounter a problem that seems **difficult** to solve. You may frown and not know how to start. It is okay to take a moment to think outside the box.

Breathe in and out slowly.
As you feel your lungs expand and contract,
imagine all possible ways to get from Point A to Point B ...
you may **fly**, you may **swim**, you may **zig-zag** your way,
or simply **walk** and **enjoy** your journey!

I choose to free my imagination and think outside the box.
I am creative. I find **many solutions** to solve a problem.

Observing and Accepting

Now it is time to wind down. Sit or lie down in a comfortable position. Reflect on your day.

What happened? How did it make you feel? Did you feel **happy** or **sad**, **angry** or **excited**? None of these feelings are wrong. It is perfectly okay to feel them.

As you breathe in, hold your breath and count from 1 to 3.
Think about your **feelings**, then breathe out.
Repeat this breathing exercise for as long as you feel comfortable.

I take time to think about my feelings. I **accept** all my feelings and process them in a healthy way. Dealing with my feelings helps me grow.

Winding Down for the Day

A lot of big things happened today.
You did the best you could.
You accomplished a lot.
You might feel **proud**.

Or you might **regret** something and feel you could have done better. All of your feelings are normal. It is okay to feel them.

I did the best I could today

Take time to rest your body and mind, so you can get up tomorrow and try again.

Gently close your eyes and imagine yourself sitting on a beach at **sunset**. Do you see **sand** on the beach? Can you feel it between your toes? Do you hear the **ocean** waves?

Breathe in and out, deeply and slowly. Sync with the rhythms of the ocean. Let the waves gently wash away your thoughts. Return your focus to your breathing.

I did the best I could today. It is time to rest. Tomorrow will offer **new** chances to grow.

Feeling Grateful

Before you go to bed, there is a **fun** activity that can help you feel **happier** every day.

On a piece of paper, write down something that you are grateful for today.

It could be anything that made you smile, no matter how big or how small. Then fold the paper in any way you like and put it in a gratitude jar.

Close your eyes and imagine dropping this gratitude jar into a big blue **ocean**. As you breathe in and out slowly, the gratitude jar bobs up and down peacefully with the gentle ocean waves, filled with things that make you **happy**.

Thank you for the air. Thank you for the water. Thank you for my friends. Thank you for my family. Thank you for the healthy food. Thank you for my ability to help others. Thank you for my growth. Thank you for an amazing day.

Sweet Dreams

It is time to **rest** your body and your mind.

Close your eyes. Breathe in and out slowly, like the little **stars** twinkling in the night sky. Hold a fluffy pillow or a beloved teddy bear. Inhale deeply and squeeze your arms tightly around your pillow or teddy. Hold your breath for 3 seconds, then release and exhale. Imagine giving a **hug** to everyone you love.

Goodnight, I know I am **loved**.

Words for Parents and Caregivers

As many of us know, meditation is a mindful way to bring inner peace and balance into our day. It can be practiced anytime, anywhere. Find a joyous, tranquil moment to take a break and focus our breathing and attention on a singular thing— an image, an idea, or our breath. This book focuses on introducing little ones to meditating throughout their day.

While traditional meditation focuses on breathing and observing one's inner state, this book aims to be an introduction to meditation for little ones. Pictures are provided, which children can use to inspire their visualization. This book focuses on positive, natural metaphors and images that are soothing for young minds (and minds of all ages!). From the rising sun, to the moon's glow before bedtime, you can join your children on their journey into meditation. We hope you enjoy it! Remind your little ones that it is normal for their mind to wander during meditation. When this happens, gently return their focus on their breathing and the visualization images provided in this book. And remember, meditation is simply a journey!

As part of their journey into meditation, we have also included a special section focused on gratitude. This "attitude of gratitude" practice allows children to express their appreciation to family and friends. Meditation is not only about keeping a clear mind, but also about being able to label or identify our emotions without judging them. Encouraging positive emotions, like gratitude, allows children to see how feeling good about things they already have, can help them feel happier and better about themselves. This means kids can adopt a healthy, positive habit that reinforces kindness towards others. And at the same time, children feel how this positive emotion opens their world to compassion, charity, and overall openness to others.

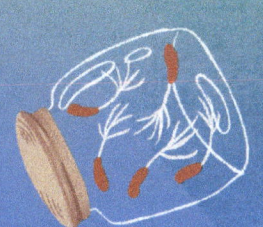

www.ingramcontent.com/pod-product-compliance
Lightning Source LLC
Chambersburg PA
CBHW041231240426

43673CB00010B/311